Broken Biscuits

June Portlock

First published 1997 by:
Diamond Twig
5 Bentinck Road
Newcastle upon Tyne
NE4 6UT
Tel/Fax: (0191) 273 5326

Typeset by David Stephenson in Palatino 10pt

Printed by Peterson Printers, South Shields

© *June Portlock 1997*

ISBN 0 9520090 2 1

Diamond Twig acknowledges the
financial assistance of Northern Arts

for Mam and Dad

Acknowledgements

Acknowledgements are due to the editors of the following publications, broadcasts and exhibitions in which some of these poems have appeared: *Lateral Moves* (Feb 1996); *The Poet's Stage* (May 1995); *And God Created Woman* (Aural Images, Arrival Press, 1993); *Letters from Newcastle* (Diamond Twig/Amnesty International, Mar 1996); *Sauce* (Diamond Twig/Bloodaxe Books, 1995); *BBC Radio 3* (Aug 1996); *BBC Radio Cleveland* (1993); *The Poetry Wall* (Udale, 1995); Blakelaw & Newcastle Central Library (1996/7); *Frocks I Have Loved* (Buddle Arts Centre, Wallsend, 1995); *Memories* (Gateshead Central and Branch Libraries, 1996).

'Washing and Worries' was the winner of the Vane Tempest Poetry Prize, 1993.

Contents

- 9   Love Songs and Long Hair
- 10 Sir Edmund Hilary and Sherpa Tenzing could do this
- 12 Sunday
- 14 What Dreams?
- 16 Bath Time
- 18 Works Tedium
- 20 Buttons and Braces
- 21 It's a Long Way from Biarritz to Wallsend
- 22 Choosing Red
- 23 Lines
- 24 Petals in November
- 25 'One Hundred and Eighty!'
- 26 Goliath
- 28 Dear Milkman
- 30 Cry-Baby
- 32 The Game
- 34 Semi-Detached Hero
- 35 The Anderson Shelter
- 36 High Speed Railing
- 38 Whipcrackaway
- 40 Broken Biscuits
- 42 Not Like Romance
- 43 Mr. Right
- 44 Washing and Worries
- 46 Carlin, Palm, Paste Egg Day
- 47 The Colour of her Hair

As a child I didn't aspire to be a writer. I wanted to sing. I longed to be Doris Day or Deanna Durban. This would have proved difficult as I really can't sing. I'd like to talk of the stories, poems and plays I wrote, prodigy-like, at an early age. I can see it now, simple naive adventures housed in rough lined notebooks bought at the corner shop, a Geordie Jo March, but I didn't write, I read.

From the moment I first traced the pastel strip on the edge of page one in 'Janet and John' I read. I didn't discriminate, enjoying 'The Wind in the Willows' and the adventures of 'The Famous Five' equally. I read before bed, on rainy days, and sitting on the lavatory. If there was something with text on it, I read it. One neighbour assured my Mother I would develop a brain tumour if I wasn't constrained in my reading habits. There was talk of head-aches and loss of sight. My Mother ignored it, and I kept on reading.

When I left school at fifteen I slaved over a shop counter, a typewriter and three years pretending to be a nurse while I bled blood donors of the obligatory pint. (No jokes about empty arms please!) I went to 'the pictures,' danced to the Beatles, giggled in corners, watched T.V. and I read. For some reason I didn't read teenage fiction, or women's magazines. I jumped straight into Steinbeck and Orwell and Shaw. I went to night classes for the qualifications my secondary school hadn't provided, training college, and spent nineteen years teaching.

During this time I had a peculiar dream. I was driven to write it down. Every morning on my first half-hour leg of my journey to school I wrote a few hundred words. Then my bus was replaced by a shorter bus journey and a ten minute Metro ride. Not enough time to write, or even read prose. (Unless you want to miss your stop – but that's another story.) Not long enough for prose but long enough to read a poem. So I read poetry.

When I left teaching I finished the story I'd begun. I didn't think much of it, still don't (though my Mother thinks it wonderful.) It was a new year and my sister saw an advert for a writing course she wanted to attend. 'Fancy coming?' she said. It was a six week course run by Gateshead Libraries and Arts based around the exhibition 'A Woman's Art is Never Done', in The Shipcote Museum and Gallery. Julia Darling lead the sessions and they proved to be addictive. When the six weeks were completed Gateshead Libraries kindly continued the sessions, first with Julia, then with the novelist, Fiona Cooper. A few years on and I haven't stopped writing. I've attended many different writing groups and learnt a great deal. My dreams used to be performing Aida or singing along with Elton John, but these days I'd like my writing to sing a little. Now that's a good idea for a poem.

June Portlock

Love Songs and Long Hair

Perhaps she will slouch among the spilled stuffing
of the old sofa, swinging her legs, loosening her hair
and singing songs full of ringlets, ruffles and lace.

Wanting her trim as a straight-backed chair won't do
no prim snipped wash-day words for her, her songs
will have red noses and surprising bouquets.

They are enough to tame tigers.

Her songs are long songs, love songs,
songs which reach down, down to her toes,
plaiting themselves forever, into her lovely hair.

Sir Edmund Hillary and Sherpa Tenzing could do this

'If you weren't such a baby…'

Clenching the cold rail, clenching my teeth
with cousin Alice, cupped fast behind.
I am learning trembling steps,
side skewing lurches where
the zing of the wind plays round and about the slidey.

'Go on, take another step!'

Rough and rusty places break through
the flaking forest green where my hands hold.
Kaleidoscopes of gravel
play teapot lids beneath my feet,
and I am high, hill high
but oh, with a mountain ahead.

'Hurry up!…'

Getting one leg over the top is impossible.
My gawky chicken legs won't move.
My arms are as stiff as a shugee boat swing
and I cannot let go. I must stay here forever,
shakily ever after
the wind blowing cold blue Snow Queen stories.

*'You're not stuck, you're **not**…'*

Sir Edmund Hillary and Sherpa Tenzing
could do this,
a summit smile with a Union Jack
at the top of the top of the world mountain
and nothing left but a descending slide.

Sunday

There were only fine days, high and bright,
skirting the river bank with the stink of the water
and the weeds I'd collect to take home.
Coltsfoot, Ox-eye daisy, yellow Ragwort
and sultry spikes of Rosebay Willow Herb.

Through the allotments my neck was a perfect crane.
Me Dad would give me a bunk-up to see
cabbages all in a row, or Dahlias dressed-up
in paper bags, with staked and straw stuffed jam-jars
balanced like fairground coconuts around them.

The men were strange; sectarian.
Pigeon men, leek men, chrysanthemum men.
Staring down with dewy eyes and bloodshot noses.
Sleeves flapped in the wind, and I learned
the power of a smile through gratis turnips, lettuce,
and threepenny bits in my palm.
Then the soft snouts of pigs. Knowing eyes
and piglets clamped to the sows middle
squeaking like chalk against a board when the nipple
    slipped.
And the delight of striped lofts. Circling flocks above us;
the metallic shake of grain and a furious flapping,
better than pillow-fights for a flurry of unseasonable
    snow.

We passed the Church School Yard.
Little girls walking prayerfully like wedding day women.
Flowers and bibles and veils. I practised with 'Heidi'
and my Dad's best hanky, but suggesting I join them
met a quick hoist and hurry home for dinner.

What Dreams?

There was something shocking
in the way she sat with her tea spilled
over her lemon crocheted top
and the cup still hooked on her finger.

Her head hung loose as the pom-poms
on the bairns' hat;
her feet, slippered in best M&S mustard and purple,
came to meet one another in wild abandon.

Him from next door had only
come to ask her to turn it down,
but it seemed that the blaring of the TV
was just a lullaby.

He tried tapping. Then knocked.
Then banged. Soon he and him
from two doors down were braying
fit to wake the dead, but it didn't wake her.

Somebody who knew the number tried
ringing, and with the knocking and the
banging and the ringing they began
to take fright and summoned an ambulance.

Then he got the idea of loosening
the bolts on the back door with a sledge hammer.

Boom! Boom!
It unhinged the neighbourhood.

Heads craned through windows
some spilled round doors muttering, knowing
she had a bad heart and
'well, you never knew did you?'

Boom! Boom!
It was enough to open any door,
but it didn't. Only the glass door pane fell,
splintered like a cursed mirror for seven years
and started by cutting his leg open,
so he went off to A & E in a taxi.
Eventually they reached through the starred gap
freed the battered door from abuse.

Right as stottin' rain
she stormed toward them.
'What the hell's going on!'
Then the ambulance arrived.

Bath Time

Every day me Mam sets to with a scrubber
and me Dad's o!d unders cut down.
Our kitchen smells like the swimming baths.
The wood of the drainer is scared white,
the yard swilled and the front door-step sand-stoned
like the tide has just gone out.

Seven o'clock is bath time.
Me at one end
and me sister at the other.
We survive eye-stinging rinses,
learn breath-holding techniques,
and rehearse submarine incidents.
After making faint saffron coloured clouds under the
    water
we bump the tin sides to see the water shiver
under it's skin.

Soon we are smelling of Fairy soap
and rubbed comradely red,
wear our fresh flannelette pyjamas
printed with rosebuds or kittens
or rabbits hiding behind a blur of shrubs.

Then comes the inspection.
Newspaper on the floor and a nitty comb in her hand
Mam rolls my head forward.

Fingers twitch around our ears, especially the ears,
and we are victims of scalping
with every furious lunge at unsuspecting specks of
    dandruff;

but then, oh, soon forgotten…
watching the bath tipped.
A flood, a real deluge,
making a Niagara of the back-yard steps.

Works Tedium

Like a physical blow,
the thump of two hundred machines
switched on every morning
at eight-fifteen precisely.
Better than Einstein we know time
as four hundred eyes look up at the clock.

But we shouldn't look out, (or up at the clock),
it makes no matter that rain falls or winds blow
we must continue tapping out our heavy rhythm
    until time
measured tells us, our machines
when we can stop precisely
at ten-thirty every morning.

From hour to hour it's a long morning
from minute to minute we glance up at the clock
knowing without a doubt precisely
when we can with a determined blow
turn off the demon machine,
drink coffee and chat for a time.

We are slaves, and yet there must come a time
some day, some afternoon, some morning
when we will revolt, destroy the machines
and reaching up knock down the clock.
What a strike for freedom, what a blow
that would be, how would it feel precisely?

And I dream as I type precisely
at least it helps to pass the time
and I work on automatic – blow!
that's the third mistake I've made this morning
hope that the supervisor doesn't clock
what I'm doing, I'm not really a machine.

I leave them all behind me, machines,
supervisors, and I never know precisely
what happens to them. The clock?
Is it discarded when at last the time
comes? Some blessed morning
when the wind, technology, moves in
and it all goes with one great blow.

Buttons and Braces

I'm looking for a man
with buttoned-up flies.
You see, I know that men really seem to go
for wanton states of undress in women.
Basque, suspenders, garters, stockings,
so
I'm looking for a man
with braces.
Snappy!

He could slip them off his shoulders
slowly,
or undo the front
and fling
them behind him all abandoned.

They tell me I'm an old-fashioned girl
so
I'm looking for a man
with sock suspenders.
After he undid them, and peeled off
his raglan patterned pure botany wool,
he could leave them,
dangling.

Oh yes!
That's what I'm looking for.

It's a Long Way from Biarritz to Wallsend

Maybe the matrons of Biarritz
struggle against the wind in shopping centres.
Discarded, greasy wraps from chips
and carrier bags from Woolvers'
clinging to their legs as they manoeuvre
toddlers in bag-straddled buggies.

Maybe disconsolate youths, relieved of
the joys of the shipyard, complement the corners
of each Biarritz boulevard, shaking pockets
without jingling enough for
video rental 'Robo-Cop', ping-singing
space invaders
or three pairs of cash-making cherries.
Maybe the Biarritz bon vivants know
of stotty cake sandwiches, Greggs pasties
and the free lighter offer on Silk Cut cigarettes?
There they are, sitting in Milligans Café
surrounded by boxy recordings.
'The Power of Love' 'I will Survive'.

Can't you see them?

Leaning over crumby, coffee-cuffed tables,
staring at dusty pink walls and pretty posters,
'La Vie de Tyneside' and 'Vivre Wallsend'.

Choosing Red

Like a lazy snake
the red dress lies coiled up in the carrier.
Red came to me unexpectedly
for I reached out for lilac or pink,
for navy or soft safe grey.

Red is the naughty one
greedy, it cries out for even more red
lips and fingernails,
but I am a sensible black skirt and
a neck tied blouse;
my sherry is sweet and
my shoes are wide
and everywhere I go, goes my
shopping bag with the strong handles.
I have never much
tried on another way of doing things.

Reticence says 'Return it!'
prudence says 'It simply is not you'
discretion says very little,
it never says much
but it whispers 'Are you sure?'
And can I wear it? Will I?
Can I be scarlet?
What will they say?
Waiting, the lazy snake of the red dress
curls up on my bed.

Lines

Opening the Christmas card I brace myself
seeing a note. 'Just a line,' it begins.
These days we never meet,
but swop a potted life in annual lines,
hanging on to each other when something
about the season reminds us.

And I think of all the other lines,
all the notes in all the cards over the years.
'This is our new address'
'Jamie has a Cambridge place'
or, 'I'm a Grandma now'.
Lately, these are dead lines.
Parents, friends have gone and did I know?
Not being one for reading columns I don't.
I find everything I need to know
by 'Merry…'
and, 'Happy…'
between the lines.

Petals in November

He didn't look like it.
Sitting as soft as a sofa, bum like
a bridge spanning from arm to arm of
the easy chair.

There he was, bold in sepia, with eleven
German POWs ready to play
football. Imagine the laughter, shouting –
peace doesn't have to be quiet.

'Tommy' sounds too quaint to be him.
He was the one singing silly songs, swearing
and spitting on patriotism. Afterwards, he wouldn't
go to parades; sent back the medals with a message:

'Stick them up your arse!'
And you can keep your remembrance poppies,
petals in November.
Who can look at flowers and not think of wreaths?

I remember the spread of him, the rank smell of age;
and the songs, whistling through leaning stumps
of teeth. 'Milk-o, Milk-o. It's fresh from the farm, It'll
do you no harm, I'm your man, Cuckoo!'

Just the image then; him with only
two stripes and a bellyful
of burying the dead; him and a load of
Germans playing football on a battlefield.

'One Hundred and Eighty!'

Lost in folds of fat doubt, his eyes
narrow to the compass of the board's score.
Right leg the fulcrum, foot pulled back
from the line, surely he must tip, fall,
gravity must take him
for he is a man of unbounded stomach.

His arm arches, a bow outlined
against the fancy flock wallpaper,
floating through the stinking mists
of exhaled tobacco smoke
and the stench of hops
reluctantly splashed from swaying glasses.

Ringed in heavy gold
nails nibbled, his hand holding
with such delicacy the dart –
a very Puck of a grip.

Goliath

And I was prepared;
sword sharp as the sergeant's tongue
shield bossed,
(I had the strap replaced;
it's a bugger if they snap while you're
busy.) And my mail,
every chink checked,
I didn't want some bastard adolescent spear
finding a spot.

Came the morning and I was helmet high
brassed, bearded and brushed. And
all round the lads singing;

'They can't beat this Philistine,
He can beat them every time,
When they see Goliath come
Every Israelite will run.'

I was greater than all men,
mightier than the hills.
My name would be as giant; champion;
and I defied all Israel to send only one for testing.
My feet sounded a drum
my mail rang bells
and the battalion behind me chanted

'*Phil-is-tine*, Phil-is-tine.
Phil-is-tine, PHIL-IS-TINE!'

Halting, I heard the hush skew
from the hill-sides still as five stones.

Then; some bastard Israelite idea of a joke?
No more than fit to watch sheep with a staff,
something to pick my teeth with,
and a scrip of sorts
hanging like an old whore's tit.

I sneered, scorned, spat;
'Servants of Saul, ready thyselves for slavery!'
my spear sang but my shot was out,
it whipped into the earth and the thud
and the groan all around
mastered me.

After that, only a buzzing blur
a breath
a blow.

Dear Milkman

Dear Milkman,

I thought that when two pints arrived yesterday
that one
was for the day before, that's yesterday's yesterday
but it was for the next day – that's today
you'd brought a pint for tomorrow without
leaving a pint for today –
that's the day before yesterday,
so I am one pint short.

However,
you did remember to bring the extra one
I asked for last week this time which
I didn't pay for
because I thought you would forget,
like you always forget to shut the gate.
So the one you did bring equals the other one
that you didn't bring the other day,
that's not yesterday but the day before.
Will you be coming for payment tomorrow,
or later today?
Not last week, or the week before but the week
before that you didn't come.
I know this because the gate was shut.
But on the next week, that's the week before last,
you collected the week before last's and
the week before the week before last's together.

Last week this time you came yesterday,
I was out yesterday, but I don't think you came
because the gate was shut
and the week before that it was tomorrow,
but I'm definitely out tomorrow
so today would be best. I'm in today.

Yours sincerely
number 28.

P.S. Don't forget to shut the gate.

Cry-Baby

There is nothing lovely here unless
a train comes along the line
and drapes it in soft steamy puffs of grey.
Dirt clings like cobwebs to the
roughness of the unfriendly wall.
The pavement is full of spiteful unevenness.

Every day it is the same.
The boy stands, his tongue is a dart
and he is cloaked
in curses and tripping stares
which I must carry behind my eyes.
I have no answers, nothing to give him,
only a thin line where my smile should be.

I can feel the thump of his stare
shunting between my shoulder blades
and my back to front face spies
gobs of spit making tracks over
my good school coat.

Now my heart is a train.
I am making small white puffs which dart
from me, rasping like rough uneven stones.
Dryness webs my mouth.
My eyes are moist as blown out steamy shouts
and my feet pound out

'I think I can't' while sobs pull stitches
in my side.

'Go on, cry baby!'

The Game

Reet thin, reet thin, giv'is the ball
whe's got the ball? I can hoy it
I'm first, I'm the boola

Bu'rra thort ye war on wor side?

I am man. Give'is the ball
whe's got the ball? I can hoy it
I'm first, I'm the boola
I'LL PULVERISE THIM!

Awh Peta' man! We' not boolin' we' battin'.

Awh! Well. Give' is the bat
whe's got the bat? I can belt it
I'm first, I'm the first batta
I'll pulverise thim! NAE STOTTIN YE!

Peta' man! I'm the captin'. I should be first!

Awh man! ler'us be first?
Give'is the bat, whe's got the bat?
A' can belt it, a'll git one
I'll pulverise thim!

Awh, all reet thin, give Peta' the bat.

Reet thin, reet thin, give'is the bat
whe's got the bat? A' can belt it

a'm first, I'll pulverise thim.
Nae stottin' ye!

BONK 'WHEEEEE!

Reet thin, reet thin, wor'a hit!
I'll show yiz, I'll git one
I'll git the first one, I'll pulverise thim!

SHUCK!

Awh naw! Peta, STOP!
Th'iv caught it, man. Ye'r oot!

Semi-Detached Hero

He was a semi-detached hero
quiet and secluded, well proportioned
(with period features)
and in good decorative order.
His fully tiled smile
and convenient facilities
recommended immediate viewing.

My kitchen was fully-fitted and
the central heating of my expectation
turned up. I thought we could make
an excellent family home together
but my patio flagged
when I found he was not freehold;
his annex was occupied.
(I should have realised his lintels were heavy
and too close together!)

Now my small double front is broken
and my beams are exposed.
I lack insulation.
If only I could retain my original fittings
I would welcome

loving restoration.

The Anderson Shelter

They tipped earth
all over the corrugations of the tin roof
so that it could not be seen
for brown crumbling goodness
and there was that warm scent
of nurturing leaf mold.

My brother chased me
all round the garden with long trails of worms
and Father planted nasturtiums. He said
they would grow easily and they did,
spilling over the surface,
craters of fresh green leaves – caterpillar fodder,
followed by flowering
flashes of yellow
orange
and eye blasting shots of red.

During the air raid
there were bursts of another bloom
which left only soft grey apologies of ashes
where the pretties had been.

High Speed Railing

This train is like a frightened cat.
Anxiety fuels a single silent rush.
Only the discontented wasp of a buzz
is discernible,
leaving behind the comfort of track sounds,
    (Peter and Sam, Peter and Sam)
the argument of rails crossing,
    (I didn't, I didn't, I didn't, I didn't)
in another country.

This view is disposable,
like the coffee carton.
So that snapshots:
a man pausing between strenuous bouts of digging,
a scene trapped between the spans of a bridge,
are blurred and indistinct.
Images are screwed up
rolled into a ball and binned.

This seat is reserved;
(too shy to hold me relaxed).
Imitating the conspicuous discomfort
of aeroplanes. Facing nothing
but the emptiness
of the back of the seat in front.
No cheery ring-stained, card-playing,
lunch-eating, book-leaning table.

No chance to chat across
the crowded surface.

Only a mean and undisputed flap
with a hole in it,
to take my plastic cup.

Whipcrackaway

My Dad says, 'watch your feet!' I am singing.
Waiting for the Deadwood Stage to turn the corner,
come on over the pit heap, skirt the quarry where
my Grandad says the plumby depths holds the bodies
of kittens and puppies in sacks.
I never look down there.

Looking down to the toes of my quiet crepe soled sandals
I see grey and bleeding shale dust. There will be a pattern
on my new short socks where the punched leather permits.
They begin to sag, pleating down under my heels.
I inspect them, pull up one sock with precision,
folding the cuff neatly.

'Giddy up,' pulls me on and away from the other.
I am watching the sun play, hiding behind seeking clouds,
and behind the heaps, these black hills, there is a
    silhouette.
A plumed head? I am expecting Indians without fear,
I know how to dance, whooping it up, besides,
I'm sure they're very good friends of mine.

I try again to snap my fingers, but only succeed
in rubbing the skin red, twisting them into discomfort.
Shaking them, I sing about 'a woman's touch' holding
my new Whitsun frock out over my scabby knees.
I skip, trip, slip, but hold my head up, hoping.

Will we go along by the wall where the echo is?

I need to shout to the highest hills.
No daffodils here to tell it to,
maybe some harebells or scrubby gorse?
My sister neighs behind me, my Mam and Dad trot on
all I want is a pair of cowgirl boots

take me back.

Broken Biscuits

My nose runs and my hot penny hand
wipes back the assault;
cuffing the mixed warm stink of
firewood, floury rice, curry powder and
Tom cat.

Mrs Fraser with her bosom
round her knees leans over piles of
'The Reynolds News' and crusty tops of loaves.
'What'ja want, hinny?'
I stand beneath wobbling heaps
of half-filled sacks and half-empty crates
staring unwilling at fly-blown cards of elastic,
buttons, and teats in rows
like feeding sows.

Behind the finger-marked glass
and the random pattern of dead blowflies
the crackers, once arranged
with geometric purity, lie at their ease.
Thick crazy pavings of crumbs.
'Half a pound of broken biscuits.'
'Huh,' she mumbles, sniffs,
pulls out the great big tin of Jacobs
and weighs me up a few.

Grasping the white twist I daren't
undo, will there be any creams, any
chocolate fragments?
or only the crackers and dead blowflies.

Not Like Romance

She is not like Juliet
though she sits by her window
with thirteen years of curves and waves
of thick black hair around
her shoulders.

He is not like Romeo
though he stands sharp enough,
legs parted, arms like two bows strung
resting on fists, on hips,
slim as a blade.

And he is not like Mercutio
though he comes ready to serenade,
'Mandy is a slut' and they toast
the girl and the day with the spray from
cans of Exhibition.

It is not like Verona.
The garden walls are low
and the hedges,
and all that is outlawed on the green
are ball games.

This is not like romance
swapping abuse like love's vows
falling into rancour like an embrace
shouting about shagging
and satisfaction.

Mr. Right

Are ye' courtin' yet pet? No?
Lookin' for Mr. Right.
Mr. Right'll come along, divin't fret,
but you're not even courtin' yet!

Our Peggy's engaged did I tell ye'?
She was seventeen, so they thought,
why not? How old are ye'?
Nineteen! Nineteen, lookin' for Mr. Right.

Well, don't be too fussy will ye!
Our Mary's been married since she was sixteen
she's got two bairns now; and you're not even courtin',
lookin' for Mr. Right!

Well ye'll not find him in a book that's for sure.
Ye' want to get married soon pet
ye' want to get your bairns settled
before ye're too old – right! Get on with it!

Ye'll have to get yoursel' to the dance, man,
ye'll soon find yersel' a lad, but mind,
if ye' wait for Mr. Right,
ye'll never get started courtin!

Washing and Worries

She hangs out the washing and her worries.
It's a good day for it, sunny, windy,
enticing the creased cares of pillow cases
a full-blown sail of a sheet
and his best white shirt into a lively tribal dance
praying,
not for rain but for better times.
The shirt sleeve waves, willing her into a fight
with the load of tangled times.
Got to get it all out, get it dried, sorted,
smooth out the uneasy crows-feet of creases
fold away dissatisfaction and trap it
in the airing cupboard with all the other
bitterness; remember the strike?

The work-a-day jeans hang stiffly
sobbing blue regretful tears.
These men can't walk straight without
grains of black dust along their seams.
They are bent into twisted shapes by market forces.
Crushed this much it'll take more than
an iron and willing fingers to undo.

'Hi-ya!' draws her to the fence
no boundary, but bound with a shared knowing
they stand and talk.
'What'll yours do? Take the pay-off?'
'Take the money and run! Where to?'

She sees a tee-shirt, her own
alone, red and defiant it swells in full rage
and beats the air for beating it
strongly and soundly.

Carlin, Palm, Paste Egg Day

Onion skins and tea-leaves were as ordinary
as sand-shoes from Woolies, they weren't our Adidas,
Reebok. Never enough to sponsor smooth rolling
prestigious paste eggs.

Pots of poster paint were luxury. Crayons wouldn't.
Usually we scrubbed unsuccessfully
at flat tinny colour boxes. Christmas remains.
Oblongs of old holed puddles of watercolour.

Burnt sienna, umber, cinnabar, saffron. Tints with a taste
for adventure like 'once there was'
and 'far, far away'. Making smiling faces, patterns
of spots or stripes, and once the Union Jack.

We knew the right kind of slope.
Not too high, not too tussocky, no holes,
nettles or thorns. Something that had been
cut – the bowling green of green hills.

Ours rose up in the park, whipped into shape
crowned and cropped regularly by the municipal
mowing machine, (spitting grass like insults).
It was the king of the bankies.

Came *the* Sunday,
'Tid, Mid, Miserere, Carlin, Palm, Paste Egg day.'
Resplendent in new socks, frocks and Mam's best

knitted cardies, we booled the boiled beauties from the
peak of perfection to a cracking sacrifice.

There were some that survived, some that passed over
bravely without a graze, but at last, we,
the bone-breakers, sat on damp grass skinning
the sticky silk lining, a jigsaw of shell,

our fingers stained
and singing 'Chick, chick, chicken'.

The Colour of Her Hair

The colour of her hair is
all the red from her Father
the faintest glow from her Grandmother
the fiery spark from her Viking past

and the tint from the sachet
she bought at the chemist shop.